Best Practices

Promoting Successful Mitigation in Louisiana

Post Hurricane Katrina

November 2012

FEMA

PREFACE

In 2005, Hurricane Katrina pummeled the Gulf Coast regions and much of the Southeast, causing roughly $100 billion worth of damage in the process — the costliest hurricane in U.S. history.

Seven states were affected by the storm including Alabama, Florida, Georgia, Florida, Louisiana and Mississippi. In addition to these, Kentucky and Ohio were also affected due to floods on the Mississippi River. The most damage occurred in Alabama, Louisiana, and Mississippi. It produced catastrophic damage - estimated at $75 billion in the New Orleans area along.

For years, mitigation has proven one of the best measures for reducing damage and the costs of disasters. Across Louisiana, successful mitigation efforts are being achieved through the ongoing collaboration and cooperation between local, state and federal partners. Residents are also taking a proactive role in safeguarding lives and property.

"Best Practices: Promoting Successful Mitigation in Louisiana – Post Hurricane Katrina" represents a sampling of mitigation activities resulting from *lessons learned*, *after action reports* and *identified needs*.

The stories in this book provide insight on mitigation projects that have been executed in southern Louisiana in preparing for future disasters. The contents focus on fostering the journey in rebuilding safer and stronger and protecting life and property.

Hurricane Katrina
Photo courtesy of NOAA

It is an invaluable resource to:

- Communicate the importance of identifying hazard risks and ways to minimize risks.
- Identify mitigation ideas to show how mitigation is effective and affordable.
- Demonstrate how mitigation makes communities more stable and productive.

This publication was produced by FEMA Region VI Mitigation Division as a part of DR 4080 LA

Table of Contents

This publication was produced by FEMA Region VI Mitigation Division as a part of DR 4080 LA

Location of Best Practices Stories in Southern Louisiana

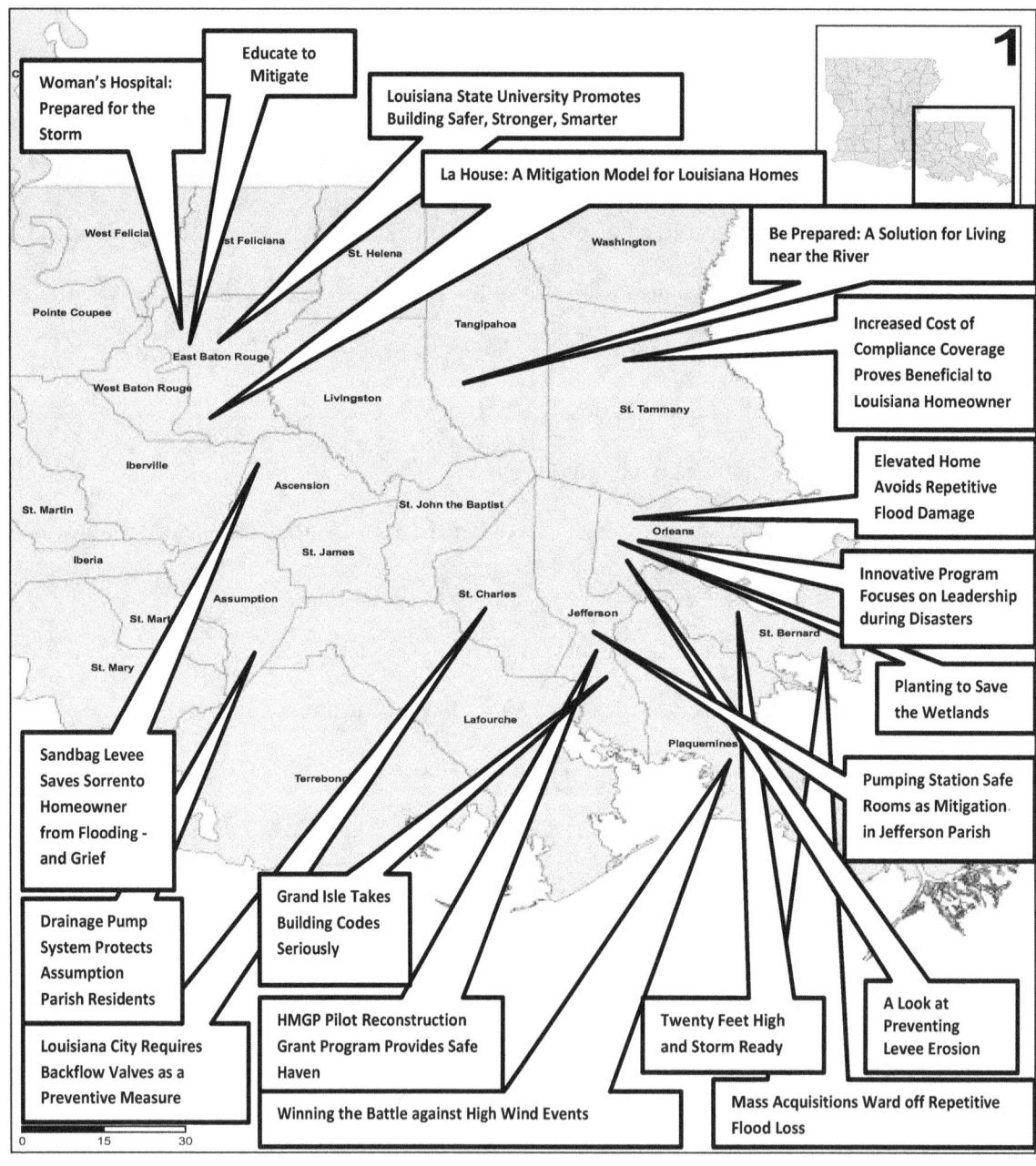

Disaster Mitigation Working in Louisiana

Louisiana State University Promotes Building Safer, Stronger, Smarter

Exhibitor educates on building Safer, Stronger, Smarter

BATON ROUGE, La. — Twenty years ago, after leveling much of south Florida, Hurricane Andrew slammed into Louisiana. Although it caused widespread destruction, the hurricane had at least one positive effect.

The 1992 disaster spurred Louisiana State University's Agricultural Center, known as the Ag Center, to expand its outreach and education program for residents — an effort that continues to evolve even now. At that time, staffers produced consumer and contractor guides and conducted workshops and demonstrations on home elevation.

Just three years later, after torrential rains flooded New Orleans and southeastern Louisiana, the Ag Center's Disaster Recovery and Mitigation unit produced fact sheets, videos and other materials with flood-proofing resources, tips and techniques. Importantly, the unit also created mitigation task forces in 15 southeast Louisiana parishes, bringing together local floodplain administrators and planners, Ag Center Extension specialists and representatives from nonprofit agencies to work and train as teams for the first time.

"The task forces included people who served the same geographic area but often did not know each other," said Pat Skinner, disaster recovery and mitigation specialist for the Louisiana State University Ag Center, Louisiana Extension Service. "Each member of each task force attended multiple training sessions as teams. Two of the trainings were joint trainings and became national events. The final gathering was the First National Flood-proofing Conference, which we hosted in Baton Rouge in 1999."

In 2004, two years after Hurricane Lili caused major damage throughout the state, the center began constructing La House on the LSU campus in Baton Rouge. Completed in 2008, this model for Louisiana homes showcases best practices for building.

Hurricane Katrina in 2005 brought unprecedented, catastrophic damage to Louisiana. The hurricane destroyed or severely damaged tens of thousands of homes and businesses, resulting in an economic loss that totaled billions of dollars. Just three weeks later, Hurricane Rita slammed into the state, piling more destruction on areas already reeling from Katrina.

The magnitude of the 2005 storm season highlighted the need for Louisiana residents to learn more

about mitigation during the rebuilding process.

The Ag Center immediately launched a campaign to help property owners understand their risks and the ways construction techniques can help make homes safer. It also helped the residential construction industry adjust to new building codes that were being adopted in the state.

"Build Safer, Stronger, Smarter" became the theme for the Katrina/Rita recovery campaign and the title of its signature publication, a 247-page book that describes how people can reduce the risks of coastal hazards such as flooding and high winds and add extra defenses to

their homes. An accompanying brochure contains facts about the realities of living along the coast, and encourages individuals to recognize the risks they face and make wise choices about building. Additional educational materials include a fact sheet on elevating homes, information on repairing and replacing roofs, options for repairing and replacing walls, plus a booklet titled "Your Hurricane-Resistant Louisiana House."

The campaign, which included presentations aimed at contractors and homeowners, laid the foundation for the massive rebuilding education effort to support long-term

Workshop attendees observe building techniques

recovery from Katrina, Rita and future hurricanes. Its materials were consolidated into an Internet portal that pulls together information from all LSU Ag Center program areas to help individuals address multiple problems caused by hurricanes. In addition to home construction, topics include financial recovery and assistance, landscape issues and health concerns related to floodwaters. It also features map interfaces for obtaining site-specific wind and flood risks and ground elevations, thus supporting code enforcement education.

Ag Center specialists continue to update the site, with Hurricane Isaac prompting the addition of new flood map layers into the "Rebuilding Resources" portal. "We crafted a new outreach piece on wet - that condensed the most significant parts of the 1995 'Wet Flood-proofing' fact sheet," Skinner said.

The Ag-Center's efforts to find ways to educate the public have resulted in successful collaboration with several agencies and departments. The "Build Safer, Stronger, Smarter" brochures and fact sheets

were funded by the Federal Emergency Management Agency (FEMA). The mitigation guide was funded by grants from FEMA, and cooperative agreements with the Louisiana Department of Natural Resources and the Louisiana Sea Grant College Program.

The interactive hazard mapping portal has received funds through the State Office of Floodplain Regulations at the Louisiana Department of Transportation and Development; those funds have come from FEMA's Map Modernization program and the Louisiana Department of Natural Resources.

"Every resource we developed with FEMA funding has contributed to the information we bring out after any flood, and each new initiative builds upon the work of past projects," Skinner said. "We distributed the 'Build Safer, Stronger, Smarter' publications through our online system and physical copies following Hurricane Isaac."

Additional information can be found on the website at www.LSUAgCenter/Rebuilding, by visiting La House or by contacting the LSU

Ag Center office in each parish.

"The magnitude of the storm season highlighted the need for residents to learn about mitigation."

Disaster Mitigation Working in Louisiana

Elevated Home Avoids Repetitive Flood Damage

Photo of Sultana Hasan standing in front of her elevated home

Orleans Parish, La. – When Hurricane Katrina hit the Louisiana coast on August 29, 2005, Sultana Hasen escaped with her life, but little else.

"It was awful. We lost everything," said Hasen of the damage. At their height, floodwaters in her home reached 8 feet high. "We were lucky, though – our lives were spared."

Deemed the deadliest and most destructive Atlantic hurricane of the 2005 Atlantic hurricane season, Hurricane Katrina wreaked havoc on New Orleans. The storm surge caused more than 50 breaches in drainage canal levees. Just two days after landfall, 80 percent of New Orleans was flooded, with some parts under 15 feet of water.

Hasen's home and the neighboring houses on Live Oak Street are vulnerable to frequent flooding events. Heavy rains and poor drainage contribute to the vulnerability. Over the years, the various owners of the Depression-era home have filed seven loss claims for its structure and contents.

Determined to do something about the vicious cycle of flooding and repairing, Hasan decided not only to rebuild but to elevate her home to avoid a recurrence of the nightmare. In her planning, the contract employee of the U.S. Army Corps of Engineers carefully considered several factors, including the base flood elevation, which is the height, relative to the mean sea level, that has a one percent chance of being equaled or exceeded by flood waters in a given year.

"I had three things in mind regarding the project – to build at least two feet above the base flood elevation, to construct an energy-efficient home and to make certain that it was cost effective," said Hasen.

After assessing her rebuilding options, Hasen searched the Federal Emergency Management Agency (FEMA) website and other resources for information on home construction in coastal areas.

"FEMA did a good job on making publications accessible," she said. "You can go to their website if you want information on base flood elevation; the flood maps are there, along with the pamphlets and books."

She also found "Best Practice" stories about hazard mitigation very helpful.

"You can actually see how other folks mitigated their homes," said Hasen. "I had an additional advantage. When I didn't understand something, I went to the engineers at work for an explanation. I also attended a meeting on what to look

for in hiring a good contractor."

Partly funded by the Repetitive Flood Claims (RFC) grant program and grant money administered by the Governor's Office

Photo depicting damages to Hasen's home following Hurricane Katrina

of Homeland Security and Emergency Preparedness, Hasen's 1,440-square foot wood-framed home has a new base composed of 36 pilings that are 33 feet long and 9 inches in diameter. They are buried at a depth of 25 feet. Plastic lattice boards encase the pilings and protect them from water-borne debris. At an approximate cost of $160,000, the project was initiated in August, 2008 and completed in April, 2009.

The RFC grant program is designed to reduce or eliminate the long-term risk of flood damage to

structures insured under the National Flood Insurance Program (NFIP) that have had one or more claim payments for flood damage. RFC funds may only be used to mitigate structures located within a

state or community that is participating in the NFIP and cannot meet the requirements of the Flood Mitigation Assistance program due to lack of cost share or lack of capacity to manage the activities.

Hasen's home project took eight months to complete. Seven years later – and on the exact date that Hurricane Katrina arrived in New Orleans – Hurricane Isaac made landfall. It unleashed relentless rain on the city, flooding areas north and south of it. Hasen, along with her husband and daughter, chose to remain in the home.

"We had 14.4 inches of water in a 24-hour period and the wind was very strong," said Hasen. "Following the storm, people asked if we weren't scared to stay in the house and we told them no. We felt safe and we were high and dry. They also wanted to know how I get up and down those steps. I said, 'Easily, especially when I can stand here and see the water going by.'"

While floodwaters damaged her neighbors' homes, Hasen's home escaped unscathed. And her neighbors have taken notice. One who suffered another flood loss because of Hurricane Isaac has sought advice from her regarding elevating his home.

Photo of floodwaters in front of Hasen's home

"I had three things in mind regarding the project – to build at least two feet above the base flood elevation, to construct an energy-efficient home and to make certain that it was cost effective."

Sandbag Levee Saves Sorrento Homeowner from Flooding – and Grief

Photo of floodwater on Waguespack's property following Hurricane Isaac

ASCENSION PARISH, La. – As heavy rains from Hurricane Isaac poured down over the town of Sorrento in late August 2012, longtime resident Barry J. Waguespack sprang into action to protect his home from serious damage – with a little help from some good friends, his parish government and a few prisoners.

Isaac made first landfall in Louisiana on Aug. 28, moved back out over the Gulf and then struck land again on Aug. 29. As the slow-moving storm unleashed a deluge — nearly 14 inches in all over Sorrento — Waguespack summoned a team of friends and neighbors he has dubbed "the flood fighters." Working in three shifts in teams of six to eight men, the flood fighters used three small tractors, one borrowed and two rented, to build a levee around the retired railroad inspector's house.

Waguespack also reached out to his parish officials, who responded quickly to his predicament by delivering sandbags that had been filled by inmates from the Ascension Parish Sheriff's Office Jail and the Elayn Hunt Correctional Center.

What's more, the sandbags were especially effective because they were wrapped in clear plastic sheeting as recommended by Louisiana University's Agricultural Center. With good friends donating their labor and the parish helping out with sandbags, the whole project cost Waguespack just $800, mainly for tractor rentals and other expenses. His insurance deductible is higher than that amount.

More importantly, the effort was successful. Waguespack's levee-and-sandbag effort was high enough to stave off flooding from 18 inches of water, saving him from days and weeks of damage cleanup and misery. He did have to fix a cracked window and minor roof damage, but the small amount of water that seeped into his house was easily removed with a sump pump.

"I just hope telling my story helps somebody else," Waguespack said, as part of explaining his effort and the efforts of others who helped him.

This wasn't the first time the former Dow Chemical Co. worker had mitigated his property. After buying the two-acre lot, which Waguespack described as a "hole," he elevated it one foot with 80 truckloads of river silt before he started construction of his house.

Volunteers transporting sandbags for floodwall

Even then, 12 years ago, he knew the area could flood. His home is three miles from the Mississippi River and is located within the Special Flood Hazard Area based on the Flood Insurance Rate Map. Bayou Conway is the nearest body of water. Waguespack has had flood insurance for his home since 2001.

For other Louisianans who want to be prepared as Waguespack was, Louisiana State University's Agricultural Center, through its Cooperative Extension Service, has published the fact sheet "Using Sandbags for Flood Protection."

It includes such tips as:

- Sandbags alone, when filled and stacked properly, can hold back flood-water, but are most effective when used with polyethylene (plastic) sheeting. Although bags may be burlap or plastic, the plastic bags can be reused; burlap bags tend to rot after use.

- When creating a flood barrier with sandbags, stack sandbags so the seams between bags are staggered. Tuck the top of each bag under so the bag is sealed by its own weight.

- If you need protection from water deeper than two feet, the stack of sandbags should look more like a levee.
- It's important to note that a permanent or temporary floodwall or levee is not a complete protection system Have an evacuation plan. Decide in advance when you will abandon a flood fight and save your life.

The Extension's flood mitigation work is supported by the Federal Emergency Management Agency through its Hazard Mitigation Grant Program (HMGP). The HMGP is administered in Louisiana by the Louisiana Office of Emergency Preparedness.

Additional flood protection and recovery information is available from the parish of the Louisiana Cooperative Extension Service or at LSU Agricultural Center's website: www.louisianafloods.org.

Barry Waguespack standing in front of his flood protected home after floodwaters receded.

"It's important to note that a permanent or temporary floodwall or levee is not a complete protection system. Have an evacuation plan. Decide in advance when you will abandon a flood fight and save your life."

Planting to Save the Wetlands

Knott inspects varieties of grass

New Orleans, LA. - The hundreds of miles of wetlands along Louisiana's coastline are a vital asset in the ongoing struggle to reduce the impact of powerful hurricanes and storms. These swamps and marshes provide a natural buffer against waves and storm surges — and even protect people and property farther inland.

But Louisiana's wetlands are disappearing. Hurricanes Katrina and Rita, for example, transformed 217 miles of marsh into open water in Louisiana, with much of the loss occurring in St. Bernard and Plaquemines parishes. The U.S. Geological Survey reports Louisiana's wetlands make up about 40 percent of the continental U.S. wetlands but about 80 percent of wetland losses. Ongoing protection and restoration is needed to prevent the shore from shrinking inland.

The Louisiana State University Agriculture Center, known as the AgCenter, has a research program focused on the plants that can be key components of this effort. "The AgCenter's Coastal Plants Program's primary objective is to develop improved varieties of plants used for coastal restoration," said Carrie Knott, assistant professor at the School of Plant,

Environmental and Soil Sciences.

Knott's work is centered on smooth cordgrass, which is prevalent in Louisiana's salt marshes, and sea oats, which are used to develop sand dunes on beaches.

"Smooth cordgrass is salt-tolerant and has proven to be effective in slowing down surges and hurricanes and is used in restoration projects throughout Louisiana," said Knott. "It is an ideal plant that spreads quickly and forms a dense canopy."

Vermilion is the only variety of smooth cordgrass currently used extensively in the restoration projects, according to Knott. But there are risks to using a single variety. For example, a disease that could decimate the entire variety would be catastrophic for the wetlands. Knott's work is valuable because she is breeding varieties of smooth cordgrass to prevent such a disaster.

The AgCenter provides Knott's varieties of smooth cordgrass to commercial producers. The goal is to make these varieties accessible for contractors and environmentalists that plant along the coast for restoration. Knott has developed six varieties from her breeding program and is constantly looking for sites to plant and test the grass.

Another plant that is important for wetland restoration is sea oats. "At one time, sea oats were the dominant dune grass in Louisiana, but for many reasons, natural strands of sea oats no longer exist in Louisiana," said Knott.

Louisiana beaches are lower in elevation than other states because of a high erosion rate, which makes sea oats survival rates lower as well. Still the plant does a better job than others at reducing the impact of storms.

"The beauty of the plants is that you can put them in, and after a few years huge sand dunes develop around them," said Knott.

Knott has explored 100 varieties of sea oats collected from the Gulf Coast and the Carolinas, and identified four that performed well in normal environments after major hurricanes. After field testing, some varieties will be released to the public and available for restoration practitioners.

One previously released sea oats variety, "Caminada" is well-adapted to Louisiana's climate and, as a result, is used extensively throughout the state. But, as with smooth cordgrass, using only one variety is not preferred.

The LSU AgCenter's Coastal Plants program says it is the only program in the nation developing improved plant varieties for coastal restoration. Its work is on the forefront of plant restoration techniques.

"Plants are the key to restoring natural ecosystems and saving our wetlands," said Knott.

They are also essential to protect communities, residents and infrastructure when powerful storms reach the Louisiana shore.

"Plants are the key to restoring natural ecosystems and saving our wetlands."

Mass Acquisitions Ward Off Repetitive Flood Loss

Photo of western view of green space resulting from acquisition

Chalmette, La. – Nearly 50 years ago, Hurricane Betsy hit Chalmette's Village Square area hard. Over the years, brutal rainstorms washed out neighborhoods. Then came the ruthless 2005 Katrina-Rita season — which rendered nearly all the homes in the Village Square area unlivable.

The time had come for residents and St. Bernard Parish officials to break the vicious cycle of flooding and rebuilding in the 31-acre section of Village Square.

Officials from the parish and the city of Chalmette explored cost-effective mitigation measures that the community would accept. They considered elevating salvageable homes, but raising the community's ranch-style houses not only proved too expensive, the unstable soil under them would not support the pilings needed for proper elevation.

Property acquisitions, also known as buyouts, emerged as the best option.

"The buyout project did not fit our needs perfectly, but it did fit logically," said Michael Bayham, grants administrator for St. Bernard Parish.

The city received a grant totaling more than $10 million from the Federal Emergency Management Agency's Hazard Mitigation Grant Program (HMGP) to fund the Village Square project. It funded the acquisition of 56 properties, including five commercial sites. Since it started in August

2009, the city has acquired 38 properties, with the remaining 18 scheduled for completion by mid-2013.

HMGP pays up to 75 percent of the cost of approved public or private projects that will prevent or reduce damage from storms and other natural hazards. Property acquired with HMGP funds must be converted into open space, such as parks, and may not be built on in the future. The program aims to remove residents and their homes from harm's way and end the cycle of destruction. Property owner participation in acquisition projects is voluntary.

Many Chalmette homeowners agreed to participate for several

reasons. Bayham estimates up to 80 percent of the structures were not insured for flooding. Many properties were low- to moderately priced rentals with absentee owners. And some residents had already left: the area's population dropped from 32,069 to 16,751 in between 2000 and 2010, according to the U.S. Census.

Uniquely designed for Chalmette's infrastructure and community, the plan took into account the large canal bordering the town's west side. The open land resulting from the Village Square acquisitions would allow for the needed expansion of drainage capacity in that area.

The Chalmette mitigation

has succeeded in large part because it considers local conditions, while recognizing the need for acquisitions to expand drainage capacity, vital in a parish composed of more than 74 percent water, the largest percentage of any parish in Louisiana.

Village Square may look different now, but that's fine with residents.

Property owners no longer have to face rebuilding after inevitable floods and the parish now has a large open space for community activities. The annual Crawfish Festival even plans a move to Village Square once the mitigation project finishes, bringing joy to an area that has seen so much hardship through the years.

Photo of eastern view of green space resulting from acquisition

"The buyout project did not fit our needs perfectly, but it did fit logically."

Disaster Mitigation Working in Louisiana

Winning the Battle against High Wind Events

Photo of Polycarbonate Plastic Storm Panels on building

BELLE CHASSE, La. – Hurricane Isaac's winds, rain and flooding were a big test for the new Plaquemines Parish Government Administrative Headquarters. The building, purchased shortly after Hurricane Katrina in 2005, was refitted with exterior storm panels beginning in 2010.

The protective measures were funded with a grant from the Federal Emergency Management Agency's Hazard Mitigation Grant Program (HMGP). HMGP pays 75 percent on approved projects that will prevent or reduce damage from storms and other natural disaster made available for both public and private projects.

Isaac would determine if the measures were effective and if the move to the new headquarters was a good choice.

The verdict?

"We found the storm panels performed as expected. Winds were clocked here in Belle Chasse at 120 mph, and no damage to the areas of the building protected by the storm panels was reported," said Benny Puckett, parish grant administrator.

Like along much of the Gulf Coast, Katrina caused

heavy damage in Plaquemines Parish. The low-lying parish straddles the Mississippi River from suburban New Orleans and juts perilously out into the Gulf of Mexico at the end of the river's fan-shaped delta. The area is both strategically important for shipping and uniquely vulnerable to hurricanes.

Katrina's winds and storm surge claimed a number of residential and commercial properties in the area, including the buildings throughout Plaquemines that housed different parish operations and offices. As the parish regrouped, the decision was made to purchase the 35-year-old Popich Building several miles away on the West Bank and centralize most of the departments at the site.

The building's first floor is an open parking area with two floors above it that have 22,586 square feet of usable space. The building sits on natural high ground close to the Mississippi River.

The building's entire exterior is glass. Inside it houses an Emergency Operations Center that provides 911 services and houses the Office of Emergency Preparedness. The office of the parish president is also located at

the site. The building's estimated replacement value is nearly $3 million with its contents, including emergency communications equipment.

To protect everything, the parish used the HMGP funds to install more than 10,000 linear feet of polycarbonate plastic storm panels on the building's exterior. The panels provide protection against winds up to 140 mph, are debris resistant and comply with the 2003 International Building Code. They are delicate enough to transmit light, while possessing enough durability to withstand hurricane-blown debris.

Isaac proved the mitigation measures worked.

"As a matter of fact, the project works so well that plans are in motion to harden 30 additional parish buildings," added Hilda Lott, Puckett's assistant. "I have received calls from other parishes inquiring about the performance outcome of our project."

Photo shows Popich Building retrofit project at 50 percent completion and parking space underneath.

"We found the storm panels performed as expected. Winds were clocked here in Belle Chasse at 120 mph, and no damage to the areas of the building protected by the storm panels was reported."

Disaster Mitigation Working in Louisiana

LaHouse: A Mitigation Model for Louisiana Homes

Photo of the front elevation of the La House

Baton Rouge, La. – The hurricanes, tropical storms and floods that have struck Louisiana over the decades have destroyed thousands of homes, but better building techniques on display at Louisiana State University are meant to make that level of destruction a topic for the history books rather than the news.

Sparked by the need to educate coastal Louisiana homeowners on how to build hurricane- and flood-resistant homes, the Agricultural Center at Louisiana State University (LSU) constructed theLouisiana Home and Landscape Resource Center, also known as LaHouse. A public-private partnership built with monetary gifts and donated materials, the house's construction began in 2004.

The exhibit house showcases construction best practices and addresses durability as a key component, along with energy efficiency and healthy home benefits. Designed to hold up against 130-mph hurricane-force winds and combat flooding, the house actually passed its first test before it was even completed.

In 2005, crews were framing up the house for high performance when hurricanes Katrina and Rita stunned the Louisiana Gulf Coast with punishing

130-mph winds and catastrophic flooding.

"The house was at a perfect stage of construction to exhibit hazard mitigation methods while everything was fully exposed," said Claudette Reichel, director of LaHouse.

The lesson worked so well that project leaders decided to put a roof on the frame and leave the house at that stage for two years. Construction resumed in 2008, with completion later that year.

Inspiration for LaHouse came from Florida House, located in Sarasota, Fla. It showcases sustainable building materials and methods. Reichel learned of Florida House and, impressed by its design and construction, made a presentation at LSU urging construction of such a house in Baton Rouge.

"Let's do it!" was the immediate response of Bill Richardson, chancellor of LSU's Agricultural Center.

The stucco and brick home, located on the campus of Louisiana State University in Baton Rouge, has a flood protection level of three feet above base flood elevation.

Every part of LaHouse exhibits better, smarter building techniques, even

the attic, an exhibition room, and the garage. The latter has been converted into a 730-square foot multimedia classroom for educational meetings and seminars for homeowners, real estate brokers, contractors, students and anyone else interested in building water- and wind-resistant homes. Its meeting room/classroom has a hurricane resistant garage door.

The master bedroom's closet, a modified safe room, is designed to withstand 150-mph winds. Throughout the home, windows and doors are placed so they do not impede resistance to horizontal wind forces and are either hurricane-rated units or have external protection, such as impact-resistant shutters, panels and screens.

Most of LaHouse has an aerodynamic roof, called a hip roof, which resists high winds better than a traditional gable roof. Hurricane hardware and structural sheathing tie the roof to the walls to the foundation, creating a continuous load path that transfers wind forces on the house down to the ground. Roofing and other external materials are impact-resistant and installed to high-wind specifications.

Other features include wind and impact-resistant metal roofing, hidden fasteners that reduce leaks, and sewer lines with backflow valves to reduce the potential for sewer system back up into the house.

Along with guided tours, LaHouse has an educational resource center

The La House exhibit room in the unvented attic and cutaways reveal high performance construction features.

that provides information to an average of 300 visitors each month. The staff distributes booklets and pamphlets generously upon request and staff appreciates the response to the house, and the knowledge visitors have gained from it.

"There was a dire need for a pattern to build by," Reichel said. "The house has been a huge success."

For more information about LaHouse, click on http://www.lsuagcenter.com/en/family_home/home/la_house/

"The house was at a perfect stage of construction to exhibit hazard mitigation methods while everything was fully exposed."

Disaster Mitigation Working in Louisiana

Grand Isle Takes Building Codes Seriously

Vacation home under construction utilizing new building codes

Jefferson Parish, La. – Grand Isle's location on the Gulf of Mexico means it has sunshine, lots of tourists and good fishing in abundance — along with devastating storms.

The Jefferson Parish barrier island has endured dozens of hurricanes, tropical storms and other severe weather events throughout its history. In fact, since Europeans settled here in the 1700s, several storms have put the island, and the town, under water altogether.

"Following Hurricane Katrina, the island looked like a bomb had exploded," said Nora Combel, the town's certified building official. As residents and business owners rebuilt, government officials looked for ways to avoid further damage. "We adopted new building codes from the International Code Council and the Federal Emergency Management Agency's Code of Federal Regulations," she said.

A building code specifies the minimum requirements necessary to provide safety, guard public health and reduce property losses. Over the decades, the need for a unified set of standards became apparent, and the nation's three model code groups responded by creating the

International Code Council (ICC). In turn, the ICC created the International Building Code (IBC), applying knowledge gleaned from major storms.

"Lessons learned from Hurricane Andrew in 1992 were incorporated into the 1997 Standard Building Code and the 2000 International Codes," said Steve Daggers, ICC's vice president of communications. "And experiences from hurricanes and other natural disasters continue to play a role in the codes, as they are updated every three years. In addition to what is learned from actual events, the international codes are based on building science and technical knowledge."

Despite parish officials' good intentions in adopting the stricter guidelines, many Grand Isle residents resisted the changes. These included elevating certain structures while installing ground-level lattice work or other walls designed to break away during flood events. Residents who wanted secure storage buildings could elevate

them, but storage sheds remaining on the ground also had to use break-away or flow-through walls. Ground-level structures could not be wired for

Rods are placed on either side of openings (windows and doors) through bottom and top plates

electricity.

"Prospective homeowners argued that the new codes increased building costs," Combel said. "They also wanted secure low enclosures for lawn mowers, boats and other equipment."

But building officials remained firm.

"Residents know we're serious and we follow the codes very carefully," said Combel. "They are getting acclimated to having to

build with the hurricane straps, high impact glass or shutters. They know that a continuous load-path is mandatory in construction."

Combel works with Irvin Richoux, floodplain administrator and code enforcement and building official. The team challenges anyone who tries to hedge on the newly adopted codes.

They make at least six inspections, starting with a visit to see the property and go over the building plans. During subsequent inspections, they check the pilings, nail patterning, strapping, plumbing and electrical systems, ending

Repetitive Flood Claims (RFC) grant program and grant money administered with a final, overall review of the work.

"If something isn't right, it has to be fixed before construction can move forward," Combel said.

Since Hurricane Katrina, 111 existing homes have been elevated and 261 new homes have been built in accordance with the new codes, with more expected. Hurricane Isaac put all the houses to the test.

"The mayor, a couple of firemen, a couple of policemen and I rode out Hurricane Isaac here in the government multiplex," said Combel. "Following the storm, we toured the island. We were amazed at how little damage was done to the elevated homes. We saw only a few missing shingles and some damaged siding."

"It just goes to show you that although mitigating your home may be costly, it saves in the long run," added Richoux. "There wasn't any damage to the homes that were constructed according to the new codes."

New construction inspected for hurricane clips and nail pattern

"Residents know we're serious and we follow the codes very carefully."

Disaster Mitigation Working in Louisiana

Be Prepared: A Solution for Living near the River

View of rear elevation of the Hank's mitigated home

After Jack retired from his job as a senior accounts manager with Dow Chemical Co., he and Fancy began making plans to move to Amite, La., near the Tangipahoa River. Fancy had grown up in the area and wanted to return.

They purchased six acres of land and began planning a 1,500-square-foot home on the banks of the Tangipahoa River.

Before anyone so much as picked up a hammer, Jack spent hours and hours online looking for ways to protect their home.

"It doesn't cost that much more during the construction phase to do it right," he said. "I wanted to make sure I didn't have trouble when a storm comes — because it's going to come."

In 2007, the couple carefully began construction to protect against flooding and 140

Amite, La. – When Jack and Fancy Hanks decided to build a house just 200 feet from the Tangipahoa River, they saw an opportunity to create a home that could stand up to nearly anything Mother Nature could throw at it.

And when Hurricane Isaac made landfall in August2012 and severely damaged thousands of homes in Louisiana, the couple's planning paid off. The slow-moving storm swamped other buildings in their area, but theHanks' home stayed snug and dry, just as they had planned.

mph winds. They started by elevating the site by about five feet, bringing in 80 loads of dirt in 18-wheel trucks for the landfill elevation.

They elevated the home another five feet using12-inch by 12-inch marine treated pilings embedded five feet into the ground.

"I notched the pilings together to give our home strength," Jack said. "The house doesn't shake at all." Between every post, padding helps ensure stability.

He also paid particular attention to the roof, using heavy-duty materials including a 26-gauge metal roof. He went beyond building code requirements by using hurricane clips on each rafter, although the code requires them only on every other rafter. He reinforced the concrete under the structure with rebar, then tied everything together for support.

The stovepipe attaches to the roof to keep it in place. The couple had the air conditioning units elevated and the storage tank for the water well located on the second floor over his garage. They made sure trees were far enough away from the house so they would not pose a threat.

"I did not want any damage from storms," Jack said.

Workers completed the house in 2008 and the Hanks began enjoying a breathtaking view of the Tangipahoa and living the life they had long dreamed of.

The house's first test came just months after they moved in, when Hurricane Gustav made landfall in September 2008. Their home had no flooding at all. Four years later, as the river began to rise during Hurricane Isaac, Jack felt so confident the house would stand that they decided to wait out the storm there.

However, with the Percy Quin State Park dam on the Tangipahoa River

View of the Tangipahoa River from the Hank's home

threatening to break from the storm's force, parish

officials ordered a mandatory evacuation, giving the couple just 20 minutes to leave.

Authorities feared the 700-acre lake would add more water to the already swollen river, causing devastating flooding, but ultimately, the dam held.

However, the river still rose above flood stage. After the water receded, the couple came home to find that 22 inches of water had buried the concrete slab under the house at one point, with the detached storage shed/garage receiving three feet of water and the bathroom underneath the home also flooding.

Meanwhile, they learned floodwaters had carried a birdhouse down the river

and high winds had damaged ceiling fans on

the porch and blown down several trees.

As for the house itself, the living area received no water at all.

In contrast,all of their neighbors along the river who had not elevated their homes received at least three feet of water in the structures.

His advice to them and to others who live along Louisiana's southern river?

"Plan ahead. It's going to happen."

"I did not want any damage from storms."

Disaster Mitigation Working in Louisiana

Increased Cost of Compliance Coverage Proves Beneficial to Louisiana Homeowner

Photo of Sharon Pfisters' elevated home

ST. TAMMANY PARISH, La. – Homeowner Sharon Pfister experienced the wrath of Hurricane Katrina first-hand when it made landfall in Louisiana on Aug. 29, 2005, battering her home and leaving neighborhoods in ruins. The storm surge from the Category 3 hurricane impacted the entire 57-mile St. Tammany Parish coastline, including Madisonville where Pfister has lived for more than 20 years.

"We got four feet of water from Katrina. It was enough to destroy everything," said Pfister. "After we moved out and began cleaning up the place, Hurricane Rita struck and flooded the house again. We got two to four feet of water from Rita."

Repairing the damage caused by two hurricanes seemed to be an insurmountable task, but because Pfister had flood insurance and was eligible for Increased Cost of Compliance (ICC) funds, recovery was attainable.

National Flood Insurance Program (NFIP) policyholders who need additional help rebuilding after a flood may be eligible for up to $30,000 in ICC funds to help cover the cost of bringing the home or business into compliance with local floodplain ordinances. To comply, owners may decide to elevate, repair, relocate or demolish there property. Claims for ICC benefits are filed separately from contents or building loss claims.

To be eligible for ICC coverage, the community floodplain administrator determines a building to be "substantially damaged," or to have sustained "repetitive damage."

A building is considered to be substantially damaged when the total cost of repair equals or exceeds 50 percent of the pre-disaster market value of the structure.

Homes or businesses that have sustained repetitive damage, have incurred flood-related damage twice over a period of 10 years, and the cost to repair the damage, on average, equals or exceeds 25 percent of the market value of the structure at the time of each flood event. This applies only if the participating community has a repetitive loss provision in their floodplain management ordinance, and an insurance claim payment is made for each of the two flood losses.

"I received $30,000 in ICC funds and nearly $80,000 from The Road Home program to complete repairs and elevate my house," said the Madisonville resident. The Road Home program is funded by the U.S. Department of Housing and Urban Development and provided up to $150,000 in compensation to Louisiana property owners affected by hurricanes Katrina or Rita. The money was used to rebuild and protect homes and rental property from future storm damage.

On Aug. 29, 2012, Hurricane Isaac hit southeastern Louisiana and once again high winds and high tides battered Madisonville. Although floodwaters reached three feet, Pfister's home remained unscathed.

"The house was elevated eight feet. This turned out to be a good decision," said Pfister. "My husband thought it would look funny because the house was small. I suggested eight feet so we could add-on and use the extra space underneath; something I wanted to do for years. The elevation project gave me the opportunity."

Five of the 15 homes on Pfister's street are elevated. Every house that was not raised flooded during Hurricane Isaac.

Arrow indicating high water mark

"The house was elevated eight feet. This turned out to be a good decision."

Disaster Mitigation Working in Louisiana

Twenty Feet High and Storm Ready

Photo of Lenore Assevado standing in front of her home which was elevated 20ft.

St. Bernard Parish, La. – Life on the bayou isn't easy. But despite the hazards, hardships and hurricanes, the Assevado family cannot imagine living anywhere else.

Along with her husband and daughter, Lenore Assevado lives in Yscloskey, a small South Louisiana fishing community on the bayou. The property on which they live has belonged to her husband's family since they immigrated from Spain centuries ago.

It stands in the middle of one of the nation's most at-risk regions in terms of losses due to Mother Nature. Indeed, hurricanes, tropical storms and flooding challenged the family for the 25 years they lived in their original ground-level house before Hurricane Katrina destroyed it on Aug. 29, 2005.

Only the concrete steps and slab foundation remained after the hurricane's 130-mph winds and towering storm surge. Nevertheless, the Assevados persevered, first living in a temporary housing unit provided by the Federal Emergency Management Agency (FEMA) and later in the town of Chalmette, about 20 miles away.

Many of their neighbors chose other alternatives.

"Most everyone else left after Katrina," said Assevado, noting that the area's population dwindled from about 2,000 to 100.

But rebuilding their home stronger and smarter always remained the family's goal.

"We like living on the bayou," Assevado said.

"It's part of my husband's culture of being a fisherman."

Federal assistance helped make their goal a reality. The family received $30,000 from their insurance policy through the National Flood Insurance Program's Increased Cost of Compliance program. They used that money to pay for elevating their home. The family also received assistance from the federal Road Home program instituted after Hurricane Katrina and a U. S. Small Business Administration loan.

The state of Louisiana requires all homes in the area to be built 17 feet above the base flood elevation. The Assevados built their home three feet above that required level.

Construction began in 2007 and was completed a year later. The 2,400 square-foot home has three bedrooms and two bathrooms. Built to code, it can withstand a 150-mph wind — a feature Hurricane Gustav tested just a week after they moved back in. The family evacuated, but the house held up fine.

On Aug. 29, 2012, seven years to the day after Hurricane Katrina's landfall, Hurricane Isaac roared ashore on the Louisiana Gulf Coast. The family evacuated about 17 miles to the town of Violet, which has a levee. "We call it the Great Wall," she said.

When they returned home, they found debris everywhere and discovered a 10-foot water mark from the flooding. However, their home stayed high and dry.

"We only lost one pecan tree and the orange trees," Assevado said, plus the wooden steps from the ground to the structure and the water meter. "It was nice to come home to a house that did not have mud in it."

ever had to pay for flood insurance," Assevado said.

"Being up this high means this is the least that I have ever had to pay for flood insurance."

Photo of the neighborhood and the concrete slab floor of the original floor

The elevated home provides another important benefit.

"Being up this high means this is the least that I have

Disaster Mitigation Working in Louisiana

Drainage Pump System Protects Assumption Parish Residents

Pumping station located in Pierre Port

Napoleonville, La. – When the waters start to rise, the pumps get going in low-lying Assumption Parish — thanks to a mitigation measure that has saved the parish from flooding time and time again.

Located 60 miles west of New Orleans, the parish is nestled along Bayou Lafourche just south of the Mississippi River. Its southernmost tip sits about 25 miles from the Gulf of Mexico. Miles upon miles of lakes and bayous meander through the parish. It's most vulnerable areas include Bayou L'Ourse and the low-lying areas of Pierre Part, which has the largest portion of the parish's 23,000 inhabitants.

Starting in the 1970s, parish authorities had drainage pumps installed to deal with Mississippi River flooding and deluges from heavy rains, tropical storms and hurricanes. Today, Assumption Parish has 66 strategically located pumping stations standing ready when storms strike.

"We usually have problems every May because it is the high-water month," said Bobby Naquin, parish manager.

The network of pumps sucks up flood water and diverts it to Lake Verret, a seven-mile-long swamp that lies at the western edge of the parish. Along the way, the water rushes through pipes ranging in diameter from 8 inches to 24 inches. "There even is one drainage pump with 32-inch pipes," Naquin said.

The earliest pumps used diesel fuel, but electricity powers most of their replacements. The electric-powered systems start up automatically, while people must unlock the gas and propane generators to fire them up when rains begin to pool into significant amounts of water. All of the pumps have automatic shutoff systems, and many of the pump stations have backup generators.

Naquin said a 12-inch pump station with 8-foot long pipes costs about $25,000 to purchase and install, with larger stations costing far more. Maintenance requires ongoing attention, with pump motors usually lasting 10 years, and the pumps themselves lasting about 20 years, Naquin said.

Since their installation, Assumption Parish's pumps have proved invaluable. Elevated above the highest flood marks, the pumps ensured the parish had "minimal damage" during hurricanes Katrina and Rita and the 2011 Mississippi River floods, Naquin said.

Even so, Hurricane Isaac's prolonged torrential rains posed a unique challenge. "It rained and rained, and the pumps ran and ran," said Naquin. The pumps again saved the day. "The results again were very little flooding compared to some areas due the efficiency of the pumps."

Pumping stations are common in southern Louisiana to protect people and property from floods caused by major storms.

"Drainage pump stations play a critical role in flood prevention," noted Jim Stark, former director of FEMA's then-Transitional Recovery Office in New Orleans.

"Drainage pump stations play a critical role in flood prevention."

Generator provides electricity at station during power outrage

Louisiana City Requires Backflow Valves

L.J. Brady describes how the backflow valve works

Destrehan, La. — Since the invention of plumbing, residents of cities in flood-prone areas have faced the same smelly hazard: sewage backflow.

In these low-lying areas, flooding can cause sewage to back up through drain pipes into homes and businesses. The resulting messes can create serious health hazards and resist cleanup efforts.

Bordered by Lake Pontchartrain and the Mississippi River, the city of Destrehan has experienced problems with sewage coming into homes as a result of heavy rains and frequent flooding, said L.J. Brady, assistant director for the St. Charles

Parish Department of Wastewater. Sewage/septic systems are designed to remove sewage. But if floodwaters enter the system, the sewage can back up into buildings.

"After they put in a parish-wide sewer system in the 1960s, our homes had many problems with flood backups," Brady said.

Fortunately, the problem has a fairly simple fix. Installing backflow valves protects homes from sewer backups. The valves block pipes temporarily and prevent flow into the house.

The fix works so well that in 1983, the city adopted an ordinance requiring installation of backflow valves in the sewer lines. The law requires all new construction to have backflow valves; the city recommends installation of these valves for older homes. Since that time, all cities in Louisiana have adopted the International Plumbing Code which requires backflow preventers on new construction.

"A lot of occurrences have fallen off since this requirement was implemented," said Brady. "It's prevented a lot of damage. We are looking for everything we can do to prevent sewage from coming into the house."

Four-inch PVC valves are installed in homes, while businesses use six-inch valves. Those measurements pertain to the inside diameters of the valve pipes connected to buildings' sewage systems and the city sewer system. The PVC material glues easily to pipes, and a valve cover allows access for cleaning.

Savings to families, individuals and business owners for cleanup of sewage can be significant, especially when considering cleanup costs. The city, which has seen a major reduction in claims, has also realized considerable savings.

Installation is simple and a single valve should cost less than $30. "Any plumber can install the valves," said Brady.

Although Destrehan has had little trouble with backflow valves, Brady encourages periodic checks with "cleanout as necessary." He also encourages people who live in older homes to have backflow valves installed, especially those homes built at ground level. "It's a very simple and relatively inexpensive method of blocking downstream flows," Brady said. Having more and more backflow valves installed "saves us money by our not having to pay for damages."

"It's prevented a lot of damage. We are looking for everything we can do to prevent sewage from coming into the house."

Innovative Program Focuses on Leadership during Disasters

Ky Luu Speaks during Global Risk Forum

NEW ORLEANS, La. – When educators at Tulane University returned to campus after Hurricane Katrina evacuations, they faced the storm's devastation. Like other colleges and universities in and around New Orleans, Tulane sustained millions of dollars in damages and halted academics for months after the storm. Faculty, staff and students faced serious disruptions in their work, classes and lives.

But in the Tulane community's recovery, administrators saw academic opportunity. They realized their campus had become an ideal setting for disaster management students as a living laboratory of resilience and rebuilding.

With a focus on leadership at the local level, Tulane administrators developed a new academic program to educate graduate students on planning for, responding to and reducing the risks of future disasters.

The program became the new Disaster Resilience Leadership Academy (DRLA).

"Katrina was the turning point for all who do disaster risk management," said Ky Luu, DRLA's executive director and an expert in disaster resilience and humanitarian assistance. "We realized that we needed to focus locally first. Strengthening and building leadership begins in our backyard."

The program launched in 2009 and now offers graduate coursework toward a certificate or master's of science in disaster resilience leadership.

DRLA's programs are designed to protect communities by educating leaders who are experts in disaster planning, response and risk reduction, Luu says. Developing strong leaders is an essential task because of the frequency and seriousness of disasters and events occurring around the globe.

What distinguishes the DRLA from other emergency management programs is that leadership is a main theme in all the courses. If a course is centered on disaster operations, for example, the class lectures, reading, assignments and discussions combine to comprehensively emphasize the leadership aspect of disaster operations. DRLA's program also uniquely integrates education, research and application. The students work case studies in real time.

An additional bonus of the program is its visitors who bring global issues and perspectives directly to Tulane. "Every other week we host a delegation from outside. Whether it's Singapore or South Korea, they come, and we tell them about our experiences in New Orleans, and they tell us what they are doing in their country," said Luu.

To complete the program students need 36 credit hours, half in the core requirements. After those are completed, students tailor their studies to their particular interests. For example, a student may want to focus on public health, and the DRLA degree program has the flexibility for them to enroll in 18 hours of public health classes.

In the 12-credit certificate program, students interested in disaster resilience and humanitarian assistance focus specifically on leadership development. The DRLA certificate will better prepare them to successfully lead organizations and communities through the stages of the disaster/recovery cycle.

"We cannot prevent natural hazards but we certainly can reduce their negative impacts by planning smart, being well-prepared and responding quickly and effectively, all of which require strong local leadership," Luu said. "These strategies will save lives, protect livelihoods and alleviate suffering in vulnerable communities."

DRLA's efforts are having a global reach thanks to funding from the Bill & Melinda Gates Foundation. First, a $762,198 grant awarded in 2010 funded an 18-month study in partnership with the University of Haiti to assess the impact of humanitarian aid in the island nation following the 2010 earthquake. In 2012, the Gates Foundation awarded DRLA a $5 million grant to help universities in disaster-prone regions of Africa and Asia establish programs in disaster resilience and leadership.

DRLA's partners include the Federal Emergency Management Agency, Office of U.S. Foreign Disaster Assistance, Yale University, World Bank Disaster Risk Reduction Facility, State of Louisiana Lieutenant Governor's Office, Bill and Melinda Gates Foundation, U.S. Department of Homeland Security's Office of Department of Homeland Security's Office of International Health Affairs, State of Louisiana Governor's Office of Emergency Preparedness, and Active Learning Network for International Health Affairs, State of Louisiana Governor's Office of Homeland Security and Emergency Preparedness, and Active Learning Network for Accountability and Performance in Humanitarian Action.

"Katrina was the turning point for all who do disaster risk management. We realized that we needed to focus locally first. Strengthening and building leadership begins in our backyard."

Educate to Mitigate

CEO materials are displayed for the general public at the 2012 Building Officials Convention

BATON ROUGE, La. — After hurricanes Katrina and Rita walloped Louisiana in 2005, the need to rebuild stronger, safer and smarter became obvious.

The Federal Emergency Management Agency (FEMA) addressed that

need by awarding a **Hazard Mitigation Grant** to the state for Community Education and Outreach (CEO) to educate people on how to build so that their homes would better withstand future storms. The Governor's Office of Homeland Security and Emergency Preparedness

(GOHSEP) implemented the CEO program in 2010.

"Our history and our experiences, especially over the past decade, have reinforced and driven the state of Louisiana to the point where building stronger, safer and smarter is now more important than ever," said Jeffery Giering, the state's hazard mitigation officer. "Educating our citizens and leaders that we have choices in how we build and rebuild is an important opportunity to increase community resiliency."

The CEO program has several components aimed at educating different populations.

One component focuses on construction professionals and the general public. The program partnered with building code officials to stress the importance of building safer, stronger and smarter. Permit offices in Louisiana's 64 parishes now display posters and offer hundreds of brochures. The mitigation theme "Got to, Should do, Want to" appears on every poster and brochure. "Got to" means building codes must be followed, "Should Do" means that everyone should implement best practices when building and "Want to" acknowledges that people want to protect their families and property.

Another addresses the business community. A 46-page book, "From Risk to Resiliency," was developed and designed specifically for businesses. It discusses the value of mitigation, preparedness, planning and responding to disasters.

A third component involved educating students about mitigation. The CEO program

Ben Plaia and Kathy Ashworth, both program administrators, hold a display of trophies that the Outreach Program has been awarded

identified the need for an effective tool to teach young people about Louisiana's major hazards, hazard mitigation measures and how those measures can lessen the impact of future disasters. The CEO team created the board games "*Mitigation Nation*" and "*It's Your Turn*!" designed for elementary, middle and high school students. These games are a fun and informative way to educate students on the importance of mitigation and the steps they can take before disasters strike. A more advanced game is being developed as a teaching tool for adults.

Workshops and training sessions are also an integral part of the outreach campaign. Focusing on speeding up the recovery process, GOHSEP offered a series of workshops to contractors and the public geared toward moving Louisiana forward, including "Getting It Right! The Practice of Procurement." The "Funding Hazard Mitigation Series" is also offered.

Each effort has succeeded, with more than 30 national and international awards presented to the CEO program for successfully conveying the "mitigation matters" message to the public.

A CEO communication tool accessible to the public is the GOHSEP Hazard Mitigation website found at www.getagameplan.org that contains materials and information. Included on the website is a newsletter with important messages about mitigation.

"The Community Education and Outreach effort brings the message on the importance of hazard mitigation to our state , our friends an our communities, making 'mitigation' a household word."

"Our history and our experiences, especially over the past decade, have reinforced and given the state of Louisiana to the point where building stronger, safer and smarter is now more important than ever."

FEMA

Disaster Mitigation Working in Louisiana

Pumping Station Safe Rooms as Mitigation in Jefferson Parish

Photo of safe room at the Suburban Pumping Station

JEFFERSON PARISH, La. – Protection from high winds and floodwaters is an ongoing challenge for people who live and work in Southeast Louisiana. Shielding operators of the area's crucial pumping stations is critical, especially during major storm events. Following Hurricane Katrina in 2005, leaders in Jefferson Parish found a solid solution to this challenge at 13 major pumping stations — they built high-rise safe rooms designed to withstand the strongest of winds.

The safe rooms are 400-square-foot prefabrications with a bottom slab, walls and roof of eight-inch reinforced concrete. They are designed to hold up against 250 mph winds, well over the minimum strength of a Category 5 hurricane, and the spin-off tornadoes sometimes produced during hurricanes. All the safe rooms are anchored to 12 large concrete pilings drilled 80 feet to 100 feet deep and rising 25 feet above the ground.

Each safe room has a pressure door, a reinforced

roof hatch as an emergency exit and 4-foot-high galvanized steel guardrails around the platform and roof hatch. Access is by two staircases also made of galvanized steel. Floodwalls built about 17 feet high provide frontal protection to shield the pumping stations and safe rooms from storm surge, though the safe rooms are designed to withstand surge should the floodwalls and levees be overtopped.

The interior of each safe room has eight fold-up, attached bunk beds, as well as lockers, countertops, a refrigerator, microwave and a bathroom. The appliances and the heating/cooling/ventilation system are backed up by a generator fueled for at least five days of operation. The remaining space is occupied by a computer that monitors the Supervisory Control and Data Acquisition system, which provides information on weather and water levels while allowing remote operation of the station's pumps and

Photo of remote operating unit which is located inside the safe room

those of the smaller pumping stations associated with that main site. Operation is through fiber optic cables protected by high-density polyethylene conduit running as long as 350 feet from the pump station to the safe room. The cables connecting pump stations, some running as long as three miles, are buried along canal banks.

During storms, a safe room operator can keep the

pumps going, while an additional operator monitors and cleans debris from collection grates using an automated cleaning system known as a "climber screen." During non-storm conditions, all of these operations take place at the pumping station itself.

Jefferson Parish had begun converting used shipping containers into temporary safe rooms before Hurricane Katrina swept into Louisiana in 2005, though the project had not been completed. As the hurricane bore down on the coast, operators were evacuated from pumping stations for safety purposes. To protect them in future storms — and as a mark of commitment to residents' safety — parish officials borrowed $40 million to build the new, permanent safe rooms at major pumping stations.

While safe rooms are the centerpiece of the pumping operations, the entire drainage system (started years ago when Jefferson Parish sent representatives to the Netherlands to study the ultimate in protective water management) is designed with safety as a priority. This is a necessity in low-lying Jefferson Parish, which drops to five feet below sea level and runs from Lake Pontchartrain to Grand Isle on the Gulf Coast.

The pumping stations serve a network comprised of 340 miles of drainage ditches and canals, 1,465 miles of drainage pipes and 53 drainage pump stations with 148 pumps. Backflow prevention involves a compressed air system, butterfly valves and large sluice gates that require continuous grass and trash removal. The huge responsibility for maintaining this flood abatement system belongs to the Jefferson Parish Department of Drainage and its director, Mitchell Theriot, who believes the system is unique, perhaps even on a global scale.

Such innovation shines a spotlight on Jefferson Parish and some of its visionary efforts to safeguard residents with the best that infrastructure mitigation has to offer.

Woman's Hospital: *Prepared for the Storm*

Photo of one of the three generators

Baton Rouge, LA. – As Hurricane Isaac's strongest winds and rains moved inland and into the Louisiana capitol city of Baton Rouge, Woman's Hospital was ready. When the power started flickering at the hospital's new campus, administrators made the choice to go "off the grid" for their energy supply.

They switched to generators to power electronic medical monitoring devices, other technologies and general operations. The staff had babies to deliver, surgeries to perform and other female patients to care for. It needed steady, reliable

power – and three new generators supplied it.

Funded in part by the Federal Emergency Management Agency (FEMA), the generators were part of a state-managed project called "The 5% Initiative." It funded the purchase and installation of generators at state-owned facilities and other critical sites like medical centers. Woman's Hospital, a regional, nonprofit medical center that opened in 1968, is the designated Emergency Disaster Preparedness Hospital for pregnant women and babies.

Woman's Hospital Senior Vice President Stan Shelton learned of the generator initiative in the midst of the hospital's construction and expansion project in 2010. As designs were developing, hospital administrators focused on ensuring the building's infrastructure would be well-prepared for any crisis or natural disaster in storm-prone Louisiana. During Hurricane Katrina in 2005, Woman's Hospital lost power for four hours and then bounced back to handle more than 100 neonatal evacuations from New Orleans. During Hurricane Gustav in 2008, Woman's electrical transmission lines failed, and a generator arrived from Georgia just 15 minutes before the neonatal ward would have been evacuated.

Shelton and other Woman's staff drafted their application, worked closely with numerous local elected officials. "At every point along the way, we felt like they were trying to make us successful," Shelton said.

At the end of 2010, Shelton and other Woman's officials got the good news: FEMA would provide nearly $4 million for the 75 percent federal share of the $5.3 million project.

The three generators are capable of operating all critical hospital services. Anchored to the floor to prevent floatation, collapse or lateral movement, they

are housed on the second floor of the complex's energy plant. Their double-walled, 25,000-gallon fuel tank is elevated next to the plant, which itself is built a foot above the floodplain level.

During Isaac, the generators ran for several hours, allowing patients to get the care they needed. With the new generators, Woman's Hospital will be able to power through the next big storm.

Photo of the 25,000-gallon elevated fuel tank

Disaster Mitigation Working in Louisiana

HMGP Pilot Reconstruction Grant Project Provides Safe Haven

The Oubres demonstrate how storm shutters operate

Jefferson Parish, La. – Hurricane Katrina displaced many Gulf Coast residents including Wayne and Rosalie Oubre of Harvey, Louisiana.

"We had to live in a FEMA trailer for three years before we could get back into a real home," said Wayne. "But it was worth the wait. This house we have now is like a dream come true, thanks to the HMGP (Hazard Mitigation Grant Program). We feel safe."

The rear of the Oubres' home backs up to the Swift Canal which flows into the 16th Street Canal. It leads to the main pumping station in Harvey and is a drainage canal leading from the Mississippi River.

"This house is like a dream come true, thanks to the Hazard Mitigation Grant Program. We feel safe.

According to the Oubres, their home has flooded five times. The last flood event, during Hurricane Katrina, had a flood depth of three feet.

"Since 1978, there was talk about demolishing homes, like ours, that flooded a lot and creating green space or relocating the homes," said Wayne. "But the city didn't want to because it would interfere with the tax revenue. We got a better deal with the HMGP program."

The program that Wayne referenced is the HMGP Reconstruction Grant Pilot, spawned out of a request from several states for FEMA to consider providing HMGP funds for the purpose of mitigation reconstruction grants, where an existing structure is demolished and an improved elevated structure is built on the same site.

Hurricanes Katrina, Rita and Wilma struck Louisiana, Texas, Mississippi, Alabama and Florida producing severe flooding and wind damage that resulted in catastrophic physical and economic impacts on these states, necessitating the need for financial assistance.

The HMGP Reconstruction Pilot provided an opportunity for FEMA to work with States and communities to incorporate mitigation directly into the reconstruction process. This resulted in more disaster resistant

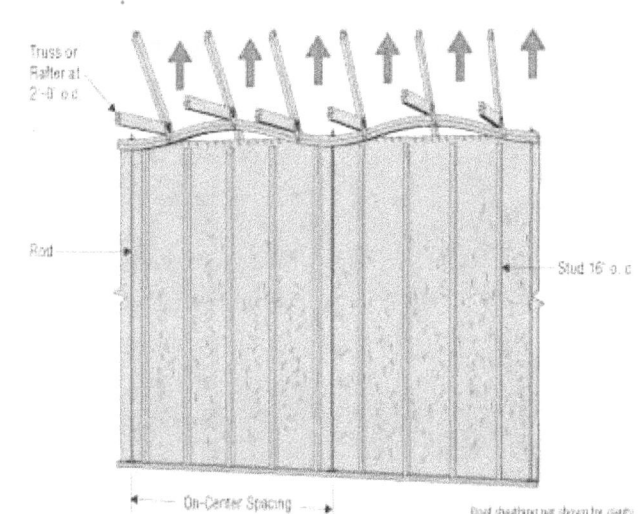

Illustration of rod system on wood wall
Photo courtesy of Simpson Strong Ties

communities as well as another option for the local and State governments that are responsible for making decisions and identifying appropriate mitigation measures for their communities.

The Oubres' 2,000 sq. ft. newly constructed home is elevated approximately 3.5 ft. above the Base Flood Elevation. It has a storm resistant roof and hurricane shutters are on all windows.

During construction a new load path solution, referred to as the rod system, was used.

For decades, metal connectors, such as hurricane ties, twist straps, flat straps and hold-downs, have been used to resist uplift loads from the point of origin to the foundation, creating the uplift restraint load path in light-framed construction. Recently, rod systems have been introduced to the light-framed construction industry as a seemingly simple means of creating a continuous load path for resisting wind uplift forces.

The project was initiated in Feb. 2008 and completed in four months. Total project cost was $220,000. The HMGP Reconstruction Grant provided $150,000. In addition to their insurance claim, the Oubres also received $30,000 in Increased Cost of Compliance (ICC) funds.

ICC Increased Cost of Compliance (ICC) coverage is a part of all Standard Flood Insurance Policies. Claims for ICC benefits are filed separately from claims for contents or building loss. If eligible, the policyholder can collect up to $30,000 to help cover the cost of bringing the home or business into compliance with floodplain ordinances.

"The application process and the wait time were lengthy. There were stringent rules and guidelines that you had to follow. It required pain and patience," said Wayne. "However, when you get the chance to look at the finished product you'll be happy."

The Oubres' remained in their mitigated home during the reign of Hurricane Isaac. Although their home was not affected by the storm, Wayne stated that there was a lesson well learned.

"We were without electricity for quite a while, said Wayne. "We know, now, we have to buy a generator."

A Look at Preventing Levee Erosion

Photo of vegetation growing on earthen levee

Orleans Parish, La. – Following Hurricane Katrina, Congress approved more than $14 billion worth of upgrades to the federal levee system surrounding the New Orleans area, including one of the largest storm surge barriers in the world. The

costly venture also necessitated research on levee preservation. Dr. Jeffery Beasley rose to the forefront.

"I am working with the Army Corps of Engineers (USACE) in the New Orleans district helping them to write vegetation

specifications for vegetating earthen levees," said Beasley, Associate Professor in Louisiana State University's School of Plants. "They recognize that vegetation is a key component in stopping levee erosion. And, you're talking about miles and miles of levees."

According to Beasley, levee projects are most probably the largest civil engineering projects in the United States.

A levee is an elongated naturally occurring ridge or artificially constructed fill or wall, which regulates water levels. It is usually earthen and often parallel to the course of a river in its floodplain or along low-lying coastlines.

USACE's Interagency Task Force Reports on levee breeches have included foundation-induced failures to a combination of overtopping and scouring (erosion of an earthen levee due to wave and water friction).

To address the issue of scouring, the USACE decided to use scour protection in the form of armoring. The most common form, on earthen levees, is grass.

"There are two primary types of grass that are recommended – Bermuda and Bahia," said Beasley. "We like those because they are aggressive and they are pretty tolerant of a lot of different environments."

Continue Beasley, "It's a concerted effort to make a system better. It's not just one thing that makes it better. It's everybody doing their part. That's a part of the problem;

however, it's not the only part."

According to Beasley, the specifications for vegetation on levees and some tests for materials used for levee construction have been completed and are being implemented.

The part of the project that's still under consideration is the research on the use of High Performance Turf Reinforcement Mats (HPTRM) for erosion control. These are being considered in areas where there's potential for overtopping of levees.

An HPTRM is composed of a three-dimensional matrix of yarns that are designed in a uniform configuration to lock soil in place. It exhibits high tensile strength and interlock/reinforcement capacity with both soil and root system. It holds seed and soil in place while vegetation grows and provides permanent reinforcement to enhance vegetation's natural ability to filter soil particles and

prevent soil loss during storm events.

"The reality is, it wasn't the species of vegetation chosen but more importantly how contractors were establishing it," said Beasley. "As soon as you finish building an earthen levee, the soil starts to shift. We get a lot of rain in Louisiana. Every time it rains and you don't have the vegetation, that's literally money washing away. Soil is washing off. So the name of the game is – How quickly can I establish the vegetation to prevent erosion and also strengthen the levee."

HPTRM's must be anchored to the earthen levee in such a way that the mats will not be ripped up or damaged by mowing equipment. The mats must assure that even if the surge is as high as 28ft. the soil will remain intact.

The combination of HPTRM's and grass for earthen levees is only one of several methods being used to increase the resilience of the rebuilt levee system.

"Earthen levees are the most implemented ones, probably the easiest and most cost effective. Plus we have soil that's readily available throughout Louisiana," said Beasley. "Not only are earthen levees more economical, they are also very effective. When you get a pot hole in concrete, you have you have to wait until somebody comes and fills it. But grass – if it gets worn down, it can grow back.

Beasley added, "Unfortunately, research is a slow process. We still have a long way to go; however, I can see that New Orleans residents have benefitted from the improved levee system. When Hurricane Isaac came, the levees held."

"There are two primary types of grass that are recommended – Bermuda and Bahia. We like those because they are aggressive and they are pretty tolerant of a lot of different environments."

Resources

Louisiana

- Governor's Office of Homeland Security and Emergency Preparedness: www.gohsep.la.gov/
- Louisiana State University Ag Center: http://www.lsuagcenter.com/en/family_home/home/la_house
- Plaquemines Parish Government: www.plaqueminesparish.com
- St Bernard Parish Government: www.sbpg.net
- Jefferson Parish Government: www.jeffparish.net
- St Tammy Parish Government: www.stpgov.org
- Assumption Parish Government: www.assumptionla.com/
- Tangipahoa Parish Government: www.tangipahoa.org/
- Ascension Parish Government: www.ascensionparish.net/
- St Charles Parish Government: www.**stcharles**gov.net/
- City of New Orleans: www.nola.gov/
- Tulane University: www.tulane.edu/

FEMA

- National Flood Insurance Program: www.fema.gov/**national-flood-insurance-program**
- FEMA-Flood Insurance: www.floodsmart.gov
- Above the Flood: Elevating Your Floodprone House: http://www.fema.gov/rebuild/recover/fema347.shtm
- Hazard Mitigation Grant Program: http://www.fema.gov/government/grant/hmgp/index.shtn
- Mitigation Division Best Practices and Case Studies: http://www.fema.gov/plan/prevent/bestpractices/index.shtm

OTHER

- US Army Corps of Engineer: www.usace.army.mil/